This beginner-friendly guide makes learning **Microsoft Teams** simple and easy. Each feature is explained step by step, so you can quickly understand how to use it without feeling overwhelmed.

Whether you're a student, a working professional, or someone completely new to Microsoft Teams, this book will give you the skills and confidence to use it effectively. With this guide, you'll discover how to communicate, collaborate, and stay organized—helping you work smarter in both your personal and professional life.

Contents

Chapter 1: Introduction to Microsoft Teams

1.1 What is Microsoft Teams? - Overview and Purpose

Microsoft Teams is a communication and collaboration platform designed to help individuals and organizations work together efficiently. It integrates various tools such as chat, video conferencing, file sharing, and task management to provide a seamless work environment. Originally introduced as part of Microsoft 365, Teams has become a key tool for businesses, educators, and individuals who need real-time collaboration.

At its core, Microsoft Teams is designed to facilitate teamwork by offering:

- **Instant Messaging**: Text-based communication within groups and one-on-one chats.
- **Video and Audio Calls**: Meetings, webinars, and casual calls with colleagues.
- **File Sharing and Collaboration**: Seamless integration with Microsoft 365 apps like Word, Excel, and PowerPoint.
- **Task Management**: Organizing projects and tracking work within teams.
- **Integration with Third-Party Apps**: Connecting to other tools such as Trello, Zoom, and Slack.

Key Features of Microsoft Teams

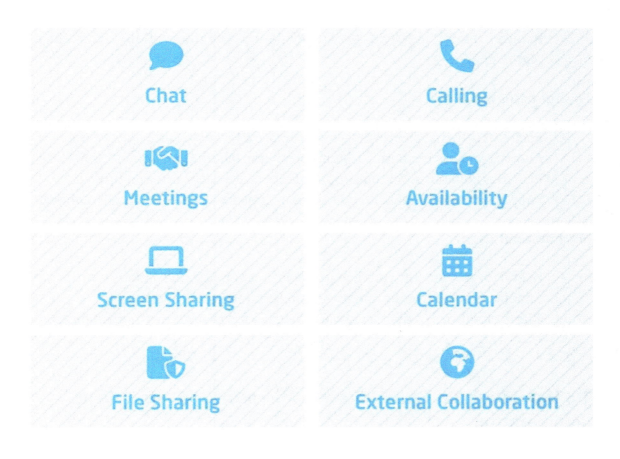

1.2 Why Use Microsoft Teams? - Key Benefits for Businesses, Educators, and Personal Users

Microsoft Teams is widely used across different industries due to its robust feature set. Below are key benefits for different user groups:

For Businesses:

- Enhances communication and teamwork within organizations.
- Provides a secure, cloud-based workspace for remote and hybrid teams.

- Integrates with Microsoft 365 tools for document sharing and real-time collaboration.
- Offers scheduling and task management tools to keep projects organized.
- Reduces email overload by consolidating communications in a single platform.

For Educators:

- Facilitates virtual classrooms with video conferencing and live lessons.
- Allows teachers to share assignments, materials, and resources effortlessly.
- Provides collaboration tools for students to work together on projects.
- Supports integrations with educational apps like OneNote Class Notebook.

For Personal Users:

- Useful for organizing personal projects and small team collaborations.
- Enables free video calls and messaging among family and friends.
- Offers cloud-based file storage and sharing for easy access to documents.

1.3 How Microsoft Teams Fits into Microsoft 365 - Its Role in Collaboration

Microsoft Teams is a central component of Microsoft 365, working alongside other apps to provide a full collaboration experience. Here's how it fits:

- **Teams and Outlook**: Allows scheduling and managing meetings within Teams directly from Outlook.
- **Teams and OneDrive**: Provides cloud storage for shared documents and files.
- **Teams and SharePoint**: Enables teams to create and manage shared workspaces.
- **Teams and Planner**: Helps organize tasks and track project progress.
- **Teams and OneNote**: Allows users to take notes and collaborate on shared notebooks.

1.4 Free vs. Paid Versions of Microsoft Teams - Microsoft Teams Free vs. Business vs. Enterprise vs. Education

Microsoft Teams comes in different versions, each catering to specific needs:

Microsoft Teams Free:

- Unlimited chat and search.
- Online meetings with up to 100 participants.
- 5 GB of cloud storage per user.
- Integration with Microsoft 365 apps (limited features).

Microsoft Teams Business (Part of Microsoft 365 Business Plans):

- All features of the free version.
- Larger meeting capacity (up to 300 participants).
- 1 TB of cloud storage per user.
- Additional security and compliance tools.

Microsoft Teams Enterprise:

- Advanced security and compliance features.
- Meeting capacity of up to 10,000 participants.
- Integration with enterprise-level Microsoft 365 features.
- More administrative controls and analytics.

Microsoft Teams for Education:

- Special tools for classroom collaboration.
- Assignments and grading features.
- Integration with learning management systems.

Feature	Free Plan	Business	Enterprise	Education
Chat & Meetings	✅	✅	✅	✅
File Storage	5GB	1TB per user	Unlimited	Unlimited
Meeting Duration	60 min	24 hours	24 hours	Custom
Integration with Office Apps	❌	✅	✅	✅
Security Features	Basic	Advanced	Enterprise-grade	Custom

💡 **Tip:** Choose the version that best aligns with your needs. Small teams and personal users may find the free version sufficient, while businesses and educational institutions benefit from paid plans.

1.5 System Requirements for Microsoft Teams - Minimum Specifications for Desktop and Mobile

Before installing Microsoft Teams, ensure your device meets the minimum system requirements:

Windows Requirements:

- Operating System: Windows 10 or later.
- Processor: 1.6 GHz or faster.
- RAM: 4 GB (8 GB recommended for better performance).
- Storage: At least 3 GB of available disk space.
- Internet: High-speed connection recommended for video calls.

Mac Requirements:

- Operating System: macOS 10.11 or later.
- Processor: Intel Core i5 or later.
- RAM: 4 GB minimum.
- Storage: At least 3 GB free space.

Mobile Requirements:

- iOS: Version 12.0 or later.
- Android: Version 8.0 or later.
- Storage: 500 MB free space.

💡 **Tip:** Keeping your operating system and Teams app updated ensures the best performance and security.

1.6 Installing Microsoft Teams - Step-by-Step Guide for Windows, Mac, iOS, and Android

On Windows:

1. Visit the official Microsoft Teams website.
2. Click on **Download for Windows**.
3. Open the downloaded file and follow the installation prompts.
4. Once installed, launch Microsoft Teams and sign in.

On Mac:

1. Go to the Microsoft Teams website or Mac App Store.
2. Click **Download for macOS**.
3. Open the .pkg file and follow the instructions.
4. After installation, open Teams and sign in.

On iOS (iPhone/iPad):

1. Open the App Store.
2. Search for **Microsoft Teams**.
3. Tap **Download**, then install.
4. Open the app and log in.

On Android:

1. Open Google Play Store.
2. Search for **Microsoft Teams**.
3. Tap **Install**.
4. Launch the app and log in.

1.7 Signing Up and Logging In - Creating an Account and Understanding Login Options

Creating an Account:

1. Open the Microsoft Teams app or visit the website at https://www.microsoft.com/en-us/microsoft-teams/log-in
2. Click **Sign Up for Free**.
3. Enter your email and choose whether it's for personal, business, or education use.
4. Follow the prompts to complete the sign-up process.
5. Verify your email and create a secure password.

Logging In:

1. Open the Microsoft Teams app.
2. Enter your registered email and password.
3. If using a work or school account, follow the authentication steps.
4. Click **Sign In**.

💡 **Tip:** If you use Teams for work, your company may provide login credentials. Use your organizational email to access business features.

Chapter 2: Understanding the Microsoft Teams Interface

2.1 Navigating the Home Screen – A Breakdown of Menus and Options

When you first open Microsoft Teams, you are greeted with the home screen, which serves as the central hub for all your activities. Understanding the layout and functions of this screen is crucial for efficient navigation.

Overview of the Home Screen

The home screen consists of several key sections, each serving a specific purpose:

- **Top Bar:** Contains the search bar, profile icon, and settings.
- **Left Sidebar:** Provides access to different features such as Teams, Chat, Calendar, and Files.
- **Main Workspace:** Displays the selected tab, whether it be a chat, team, meeting, or file.
- **Activity Feed:** Shows notifications, mentions, and updates from your teams and channels.

Step-by-Step: Navigating the Home Screen

1. **Launch Microsoft Teams.** Open the application on your desktop or mobile device.
2. **Familiarize yourself with the left sidebar.** This sidebar provides quick access to essential features.
3. **Click on each section.** Explore "Teams," "Chat," "Calendar," "Calls," and "Files" to see their contents.

4. **Use the search bar.** Located at the top, it allows you to quickly find messages, files, and contacts.
5. **Check notifications in the Activity Feed.** Click on "Activity" in the sidebar to review updates.
6. **Customize the home screen layout.** Drag and rearrange items within Teams for better workflow.

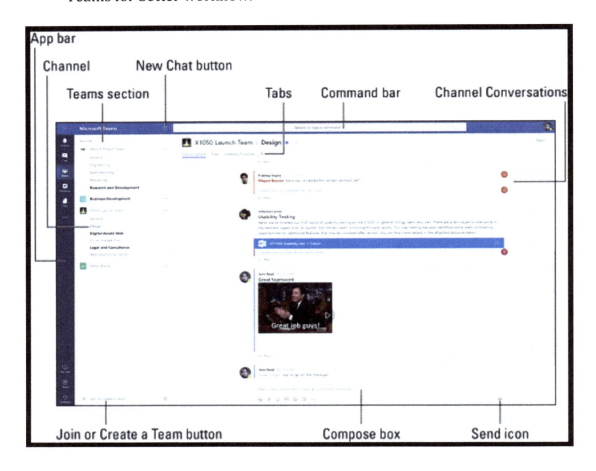

2.2 Customizing Your Profile and Settings – Changing Display Name, Profile Picture, and Preferences

Microsoft Teams allows users to personalize their profile settings for a more tailored experience.

Customizable Profile Settings

- **Display Name:** The name that appears in chats, meetings, and teams.
- **Profile Picture:** Helps others recognize you quickly.
- **Status Message:** Lets others know if you're available, busy, or away.
- **Theme and Appearance:** Choose between light, dark, or high-contrast themes.
- **Notification Preferences:** Adjust alerts for mentions, messages, and activity updates.

Step-by-Step: Customizing Your Profile and Settings

1. **Click on your profile icon** (top-right corner of the home screen).
2. **Select "Manage Account."** This opens the settings menu.

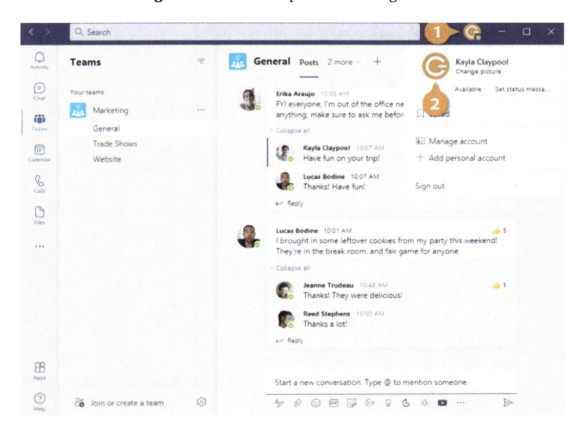

3. **To change your name or picture:**

- ○ Click on "Edit Profile."
- ○ Upload a new picture or edit your display name.
4. **To update status:**
   - ○ Click your profile picture.
   - ○ Select a status like "Available," "Busy," or "Do Not Disturb."
5. **To adjust themes:**
   - ○ Go to "Settings" > "General."
   - ○ Choose between Light, Dark, or High Contrast.

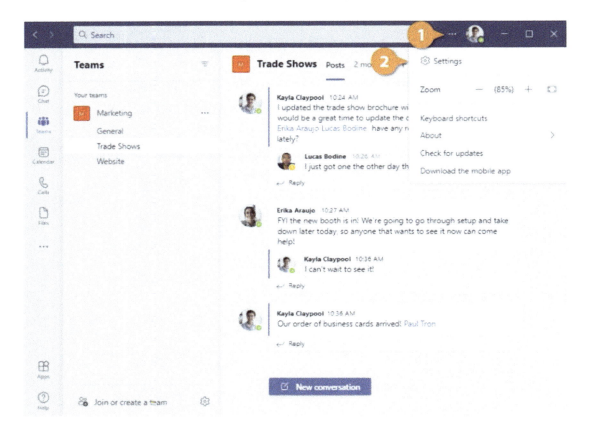

6. **To configure notifications:**
   - ○ Go to "Settings" > "Notifications."
   - ○ Enable or disable alerts for messages, mentions, and team updates.

2.3 Understanding the Left Sidebar – Overview of Teams, Calendar, Calls, Chat, Files, and Apps

The **Left Sidebar** serves as the primary navigation panel in Microsoft Teams, allowing users to switch between different features quickly.

Key Sections of the Left Sidebar

1. **Activity:** Displays recent notifications and updates from teams and channels.
2. **Chat:** Shows private and group conversations.
3. **Teams:** Lists all teams you are a member of, along with their channels.
4. **Calendar:** Integrates with Outlook to manage meetings and appointments.

5. **Calls:** Provides direct and group calling options.
6. **Files:** Stores recent and shared documents.
7. **Apps:** Allows users to install additional productivity tools.

Step-by-Step: Using the Left Sidebar

1. **Click on any section in the sidebar** to open it in the main workspace.
2. **Hover over a section** to see additional options (such as filtering chats or sorting teams).
3. **Pin frequently used items** by right-clicking a chat, team, or file.
4. **Use the "More" menu (three dots) at the bottom** to access extra apps and settings.
5. **Rearrange icons in the sidebar** by dragging them into a preferred order.

2.4 Exploring the Activity Feed – How Notifications, Mentions, and Updates Work

The **Activity Feed** helps users stay informed about important updates within Teams. It collects notifications related to mentions, messages, reactions, and team activities.

Types of Notifications in the Activity Feed

- **Mentions (@your name):** Alerts when someone tags you in a chat or channel.
- **Replies:** Notifies you of responses to messages you've sent.
- **Reactions:** Shows when someone reacts to your messages.
- **Missed Calls & Voicemails:** Alerts about calls you didn't answer.
- **Team & Channel Updates:** Notifies you of new posts, assignments, or file shares.

Step-by-Step: Using the Activity Feed

1. **Click on "Activity" in the left sidebar.**

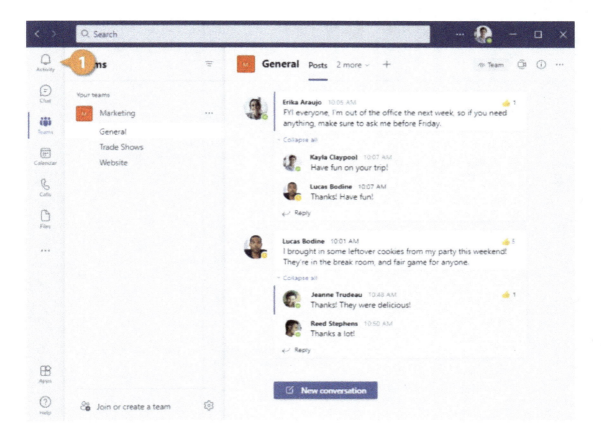

2. **Review notifications.** New updates appear at the top.
3. **Click on a notification** to jump to the related chat or post.
4. **Use the "Filter" icon** (top-right) to sort notifications by type.
5. **Click "Mark all as read"** to clear notifications you have reviewed.
6. **Adjust notification settings** by clicking on your profile picture > "Settings" > "Notifications."

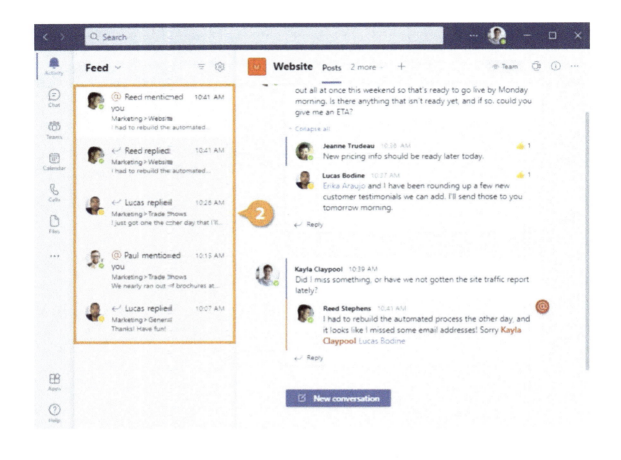

2.5 Using the Search Bar and Command Box – Finding Messages, Files, and Users Quickly

The **Search Bar** and **Command Box** allow users to search for messages, files, and people instantly.

Functions of the Search Bar & Command Box

- **Find Messages:** Search for specific words or phrases in chats and channels.
- **Locate Files:** Retrieve documents shared in conversations or stored in Teams.
- **Search for Users:** Look up colleagues or contacts within your organization.

- **Use Commands:** Quick actions such as setting a status, calling someone, or starting a chat.

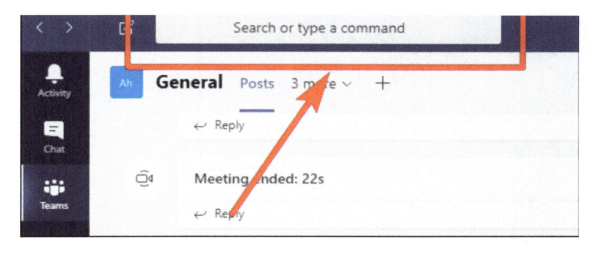

Step-by-Step: Using the Search Bar and Commands

1. **Click on the search bar at the top of Teams.**
2. **Type a keyword** (e.g., "meeting notes") to search messages or files.
3. **Press Enter** to see a list of results.
4. **To find a person, type their name** and select them from the results.

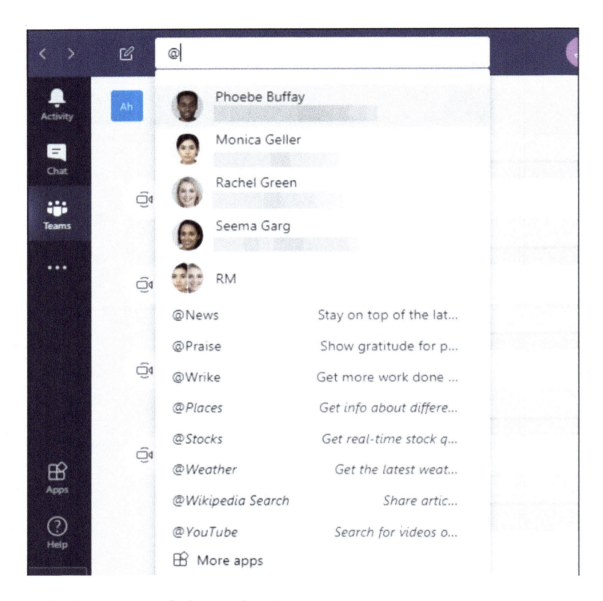

5. **Use Commands for quick actions:**
   - Type /call [name] to start a call.
   - Type /files to see recent files.
   - Type /unread to view unread messages.

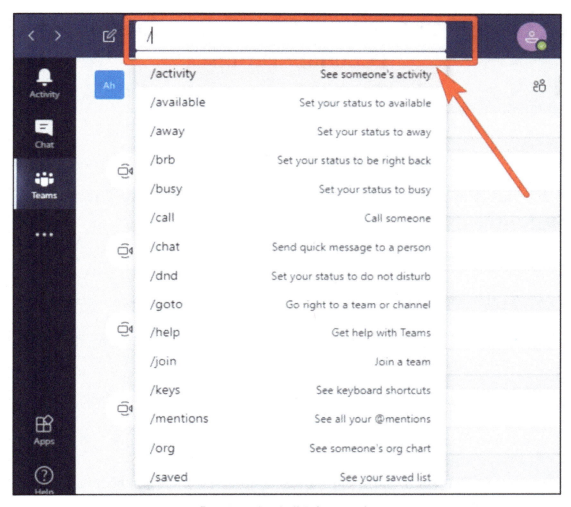

Type / to view the list of commands.

6. **Use filters (next to the search bar)** to refine results by date, sender, or type.

Chapter 3: Teams and Channels – The Core of Collaboration

3.1 What Are Teams and Channels? – Understanding Their Structure

Understanding Teams and Channels

- **Teams** are groups of people working together on a project, department, or topic.
- **Channels** are subgroups within a team used for organizing discussions around specific subjects.

Structure of Teams and Channels

- **Team** (e.g., "Marketing Team")
  - o **General Channel** (Default for all teams)
  - o **Project A Channel** (For discussions related to a specific project)
  - o **Announcements Channel** (For important updates)

Step-by-Step: Understanding Teams and Channels

1. **Open Microsoft Teams.**
2. **Click on the "Teams" tab** in the left sidebar.
3. **Select a Team** to view its channels.
4. **Click on a Channel** to open its conversation and files.
5. **Look at the tabs within a Channel** (Posts, Files, Wiki, etc.).
6. **Use the "More Options" (three dots) next to a team or channel** for additional settings.

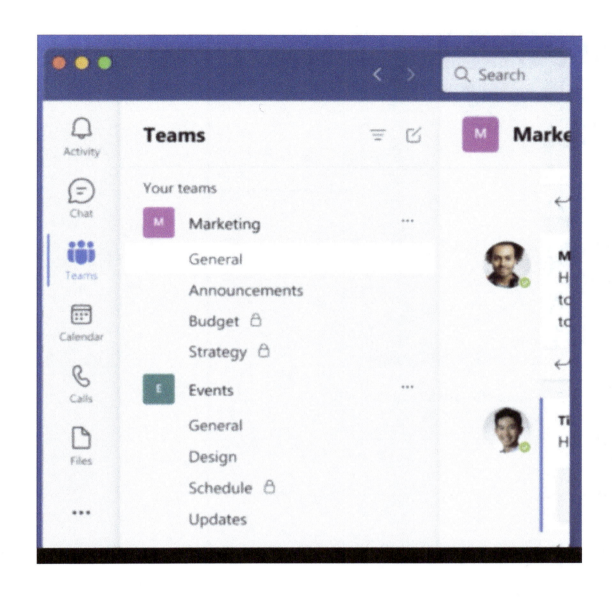

3.2 Creating a New Team – Steps to Create a Public or Private Team

Step-by-Step: Creating a New Team

1. **Click on the "Teams" tab** in the left sidebar.
2. **Click "Join or create a team"** at the bottom.

3. **Select "Create a team."**

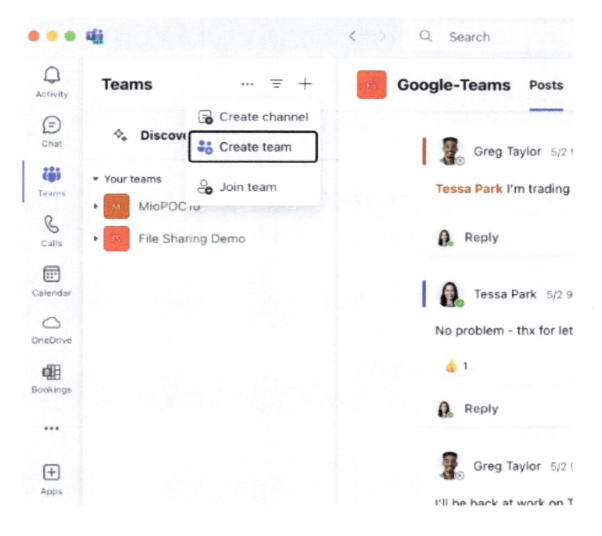

4. **Choose the type of team:**
   o **Private:** Only invited members can join.
   o **Public:** Anyone in your organization can join.

What kind of team will this be?

Privacy

 **Private**
People need permission to join

 **Public**
Anyone in your org can join

5. **Enter a team name** (e.g., "Product Development Team").
6. **Write a team description** (optional).

Create a team

You're creating a team from scratch. More create team options

Team name *

Give your team a name

Description

Let people know what this team is all about

7. **Click "Next."**
8. **Add members by typing their names or emails.**
9. **Assign roles** (Owner, Member, or Guest).
10. **Click "Create."**

3.3 Managing Team Members – Adding, Removing, and Assigning Roles

Step-by-Step: Adding Team Members

1. Go to **"Teams"** in the left sidebar.
2. Click on the team name.
3. Click **"More Options" (three dots)** next to the team.
4. Select **"Manage Team."**
5. Click **"Add member."**

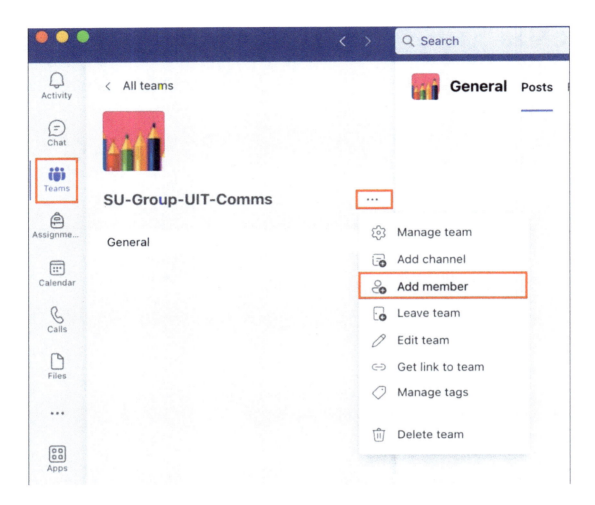

6. Enter the name or email of the person.
7. Click **"Add."**

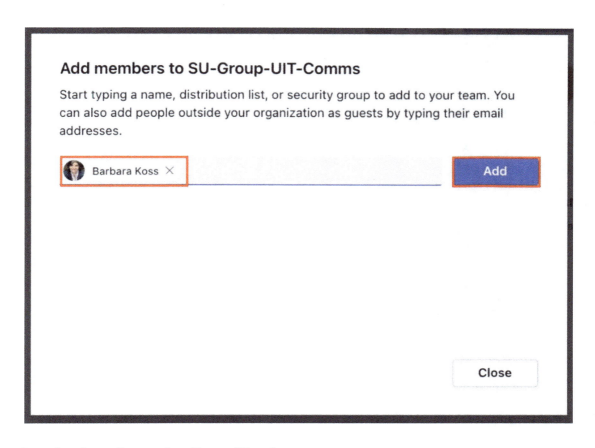

Step-by-Step: Removing Team Members

1. Open **"Manage Team."**

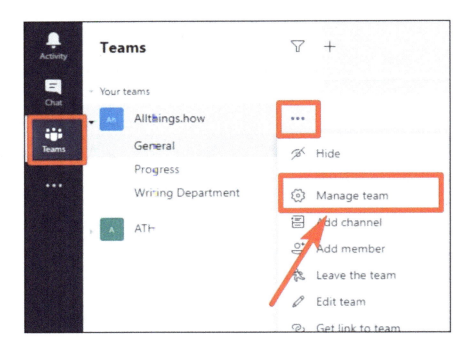

2. Find the person in the list.

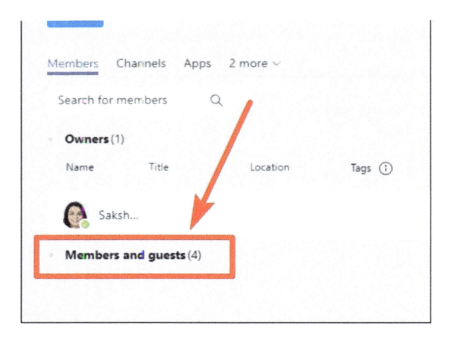

3. Click the **X** button next to their name.

Step-by-Step: Assigning Roles

1. Open **"Manage Team."**
2. **Find** the member.
3. Click on their role **(Member, Guest, or Owner).**
4. **Select** a new role.

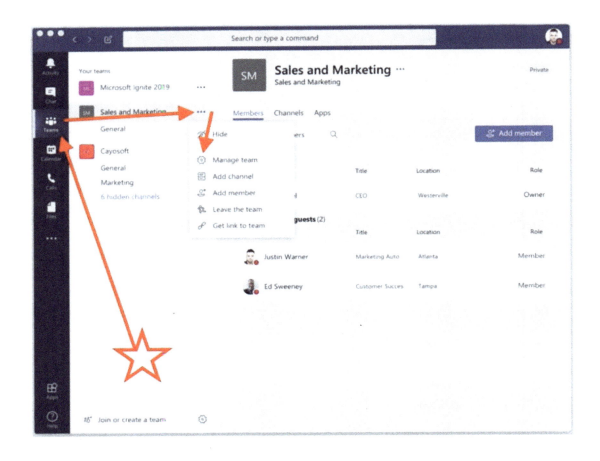

3.4 Understanding Standard vs. Private Channels – When and How to Use Them

Type	Who Can Join?	Use Cases
Standard	All team members	General discussions, announcements
Private	Only invited members	Confidential discussions, sensitive projects

Step-by-Step: Choosing the Right Channel Type

1. Decide the purpose of the channel.
2. If it's general, create a Standard Channel.

3. If it's for a private group, create a Private Channel.
4. Consider security needs before selecting the type.

3.5 Creating and Organizing Channels – Best Practices for Clear and Efficient Collaboration

Step-by-Step: Creating a New Channel

1. **Go to a team.**
2. **Click "More Options" (three dots) next to the team name.**
3. **Select "Add Channel."**

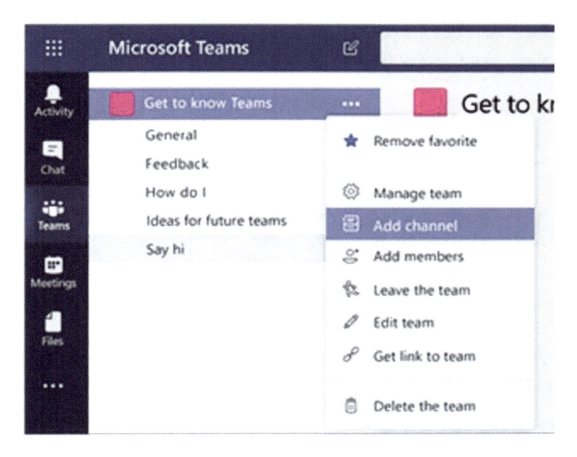

4. **Enter a Channel Name** (e.g., "Weekly Reports").

5. **Add a Description** (optional).
6. **Select Privacy Type** (Standard or Private).
7. **Click "Create."**

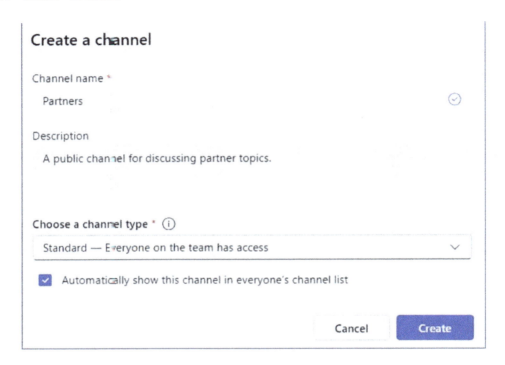

Best Practices for Organizing Channels

- **Use clear names** (e.g., "Project X Discussions" instead of "General").
  Limit the number of channels to avoid clutter.
  Pin important channels for easy access.
  Use channel descriptions to explain their purpose.

3.6 Channel Settings and Moderation – Controlling Who Can Post and Manage Messages

Step-by-Step: Accessing Channel Settings

1. **Go to the team and find the channel.**

2. **Click "More Options" (three dots) next to the channel name.**
3. **Select "Manage Channel."**

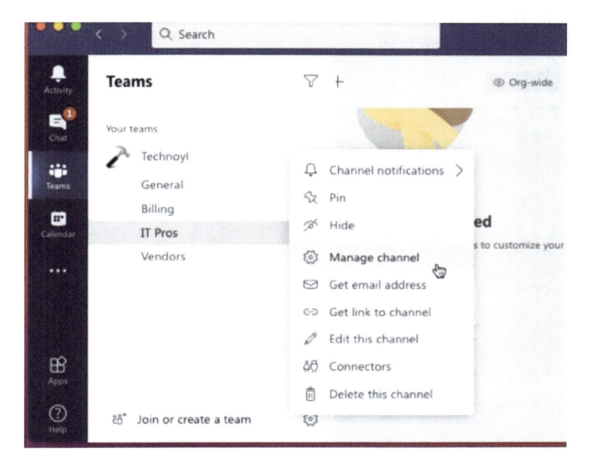

Step-by-Step: Controlling Who Can Post

1. **Open "Manage Channel."**
2. **Find "Channel Moderation."**
3. **Enable or Disable Moderation.**
4. **Select who can start posts** (all members or only owners).

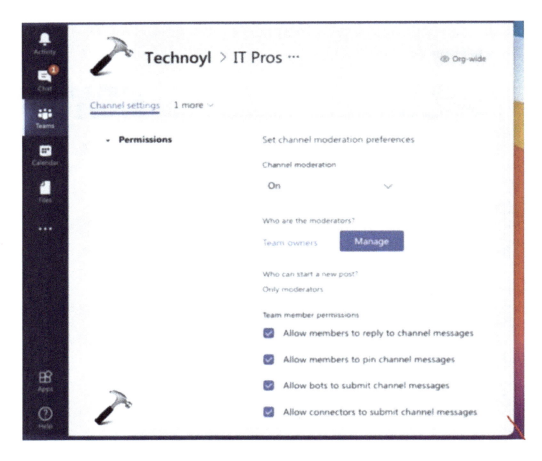

Step-by-Step: Deleting Messages and Posts

1. **Click on a message.**
2. **Select "More Options" (three dots).**
3. **Click "Delete."**

3.7 Archiving and Deleting Teams and Channels – What Happens When You Remove Them

Archiving a Team (Preserves data but disables activity)

1. **Go to "Teams."**
2. **Click "More Options" (three dots) next to the team name.**

3. **Select "Archive team."**

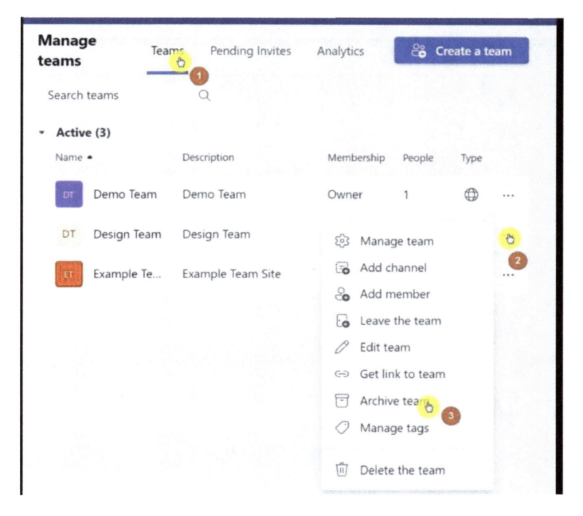

Deleting a Team (Permanently removes it)

1. **Go to "Teams."**
2. **Click "More Options" next to the team name.**
3. **Select "Delete Team."**
4. **Confirm deletion.**

Deleting a Channel

1. **Go to the Team and find the channel.**

2. **Click "More Options" next to the channel name.**
3. **Select "Delete Channel."**

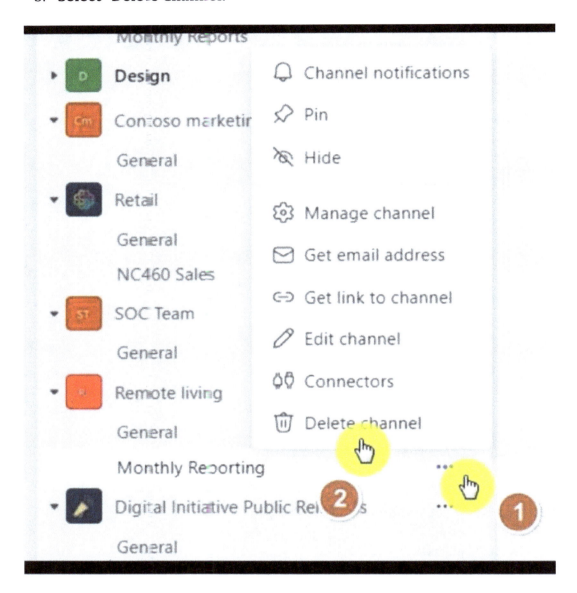

Chapter 4: Chat and Messaging in Microsoft Teams

4.1 Understanding Personal and Group Chats – When to Use Each

Personal vs. Group Chats

Chats in Microsoft Teams allow for direct and group communication. Choosing the right type of chat ensures effective collaboration.

When to Use Personal Chats

- Quick one-on-one discussions.
- Private conversations that don't need to be shared with a team.
- Sending confidential information.

When to Use Group Chats

- Conversations involving multiple colleagues on a specific topic.
- Temporary discussions that don't require a dedicated channel.
- Sharing files and collaborating on tasks with a small team.

4.2 Starting a New Chat – One-on-One and Group Messaging Explained

Starting a One-on-One Chat

1. Click on the **Chat** tab in the left sidebar.
2. Click the **New Chat** icon (pencil and paper) at the top.
3. Enter the name or email of the person in the **To** field.

4. Type your message in the chat box.
5. Press **Enter** to send the message.

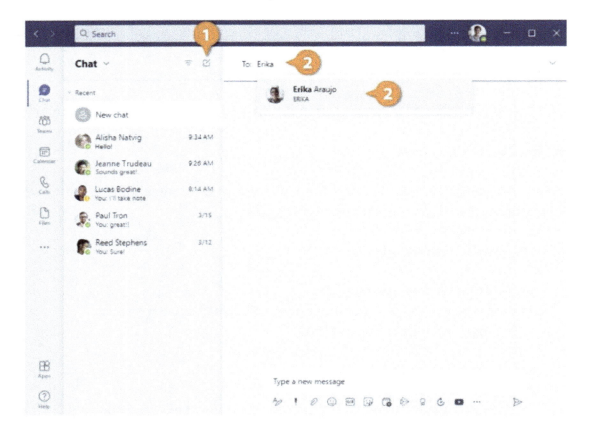

Starting a Group Chat

1. Open the **Chat** tab.
2. Click the **New Chat** icon.
3. Add multiple names in the **To** field.
4. Type your message and send it.
5. (Optional) Click the **pencil icon** next to the recipients' names to give the chat a custom name.

4.3 Formatting Messages – Using Bold, Italics, Bullet Points, Code Snippets, and More

Formatting Options in Teams Chat

1. Click the **Format (A)** icon below the chat box.
2. Use the toolbar to apply formatting:
   - **Bold** – Ctrl + B (or click **B**)
   - **Italics** – Ctrl + I (or click **I**)
   - **Underline** – Ctrl + U (or click **U**)
   - **Bullet Points** – Click the **bullet list** icon
   - **Numbered List** – Click the **numbered list** icon
   - **Code Snippets** – Click the **</>** icon and enter code
3. Click **Send** when done.

💡 **Tip:** Use Shift + Enter to add a new line without sending the message.

4.4 Using Emojis, Stickers, and GIFs – Making Conversations More Engaging

Adding Emojis

1. Click the **emoji icon** below the chat box.
2. Choose an emoji and click to insert it.

Adding Stickers

1. Click the **sticker icon** below the chat box.
2. Browse or search for a sticker.
3. Click to insert it into the message.

Adding GIFs

1. Click the **GIF icon** below the chat box.

2. Search for a GIF.
3. Click to insert it.

💡 **Tip:** Use GIFs sparingly in professional settings to keep conversations focused.

4.5 Using @Mentions and Notifications – Tagging People for Quick Responses

Using @Mentions

1. Type @ followed by a name in a chat or channel.
2. Select the person from the list.
3. The tagged person will receive a notification.

Using @Mentions for Groups

- @Team – Notifies everyone in a team.
- @Channel – Notifies everyone in a specific channel.
- @Specific Person – Notifies only one individual.

💡 **Tip:** Overusing @mentions can lead to notification fatigue—use them only when necessary.

4.6 Pinning, Editing, and Deleting Messages – Managing Chat History Effectively

Pinning Messages

1. Hover over a message.
2. Click **More Options** (three dots).
3. Select **Pin**.

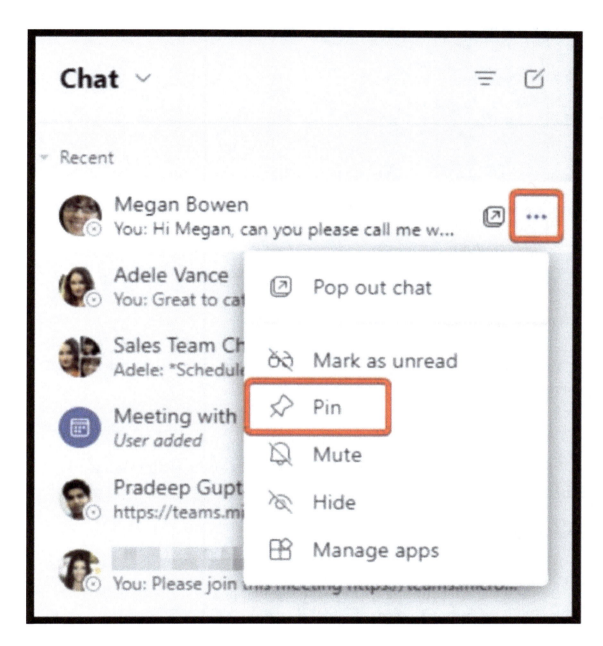

Editing Messages

1. Hover over the message you want to edit.
2. Click **More Options**.
3. Select **Edit**, make changes, and press **Enter** to save.

Deleting Messages

1. Hover over a message.
2. Click **More Options**.
3. Select **Delete**.

💡 **Tip:** Deleted messages cannot be recovered, but chat participants will see "This message was deleted."

4.7 Sending Voice Notes and Attachments – Sharing Files and Audio Messages

Sending a Voice Note

1. Open a chat.
2. Click the **Microphone icon** next to the chat box.
3. Hold the button to record your message.
4. Release to send the voice note.

Sending Attachments (Files, Images, Documents)

1. Click the **Attach (paperclip) icon** below the chat box.
2. Choose a source:
   - **OneDrive** – Select from cloud storage.

      ○   **Upload from my computer** – Choose a file from your device.

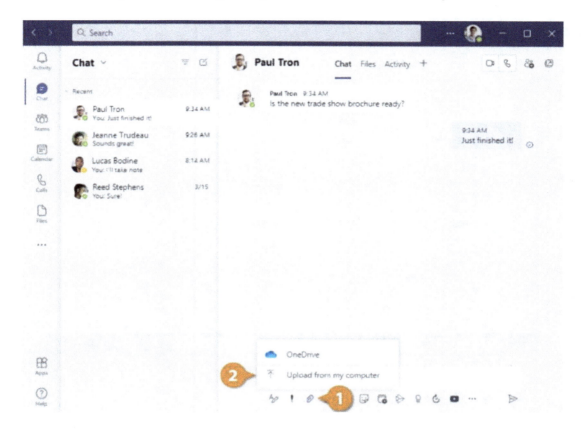

3. Click **Send** to share.

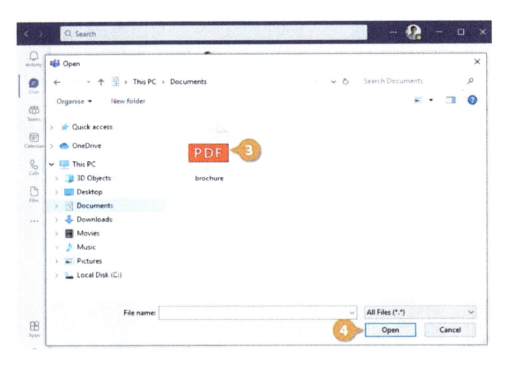

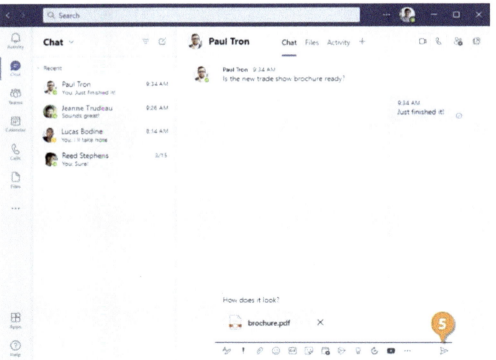

💡 **Tip:** Shared files in a chat are stored in **OneDrive** (for private chats) or **Teams Files** (for team channels).

4.8 Using Message Reactions – Expressing Quick Feedback with Thumbs Up, Heart, and Other Reactions

Adding a Reaction to a Message

1. Hover over a message.
2. Click on one of the reaction emojis (👍 ❤️ 😄 😮 😔 😧).
3. The selected reaction will appear below the message.

Removing a Reaction

1. Hover over the reacted message.
2. Click the same reaction again to remove it.

💡 **Tip:** Use reactions to acknowledge messages without cluttering chats with unnecessary replies.

Chapter 5: Meetings and Video Conferencing

5.1 Scheduling a Meeting in Microsoft Teams – Step-by-Step Guide to Setting Up Meetings

Scheduling a Meeting via the Calendar

1. Open **Microsoft Teams** and click on the **Calendar** tab in the left sidebar.

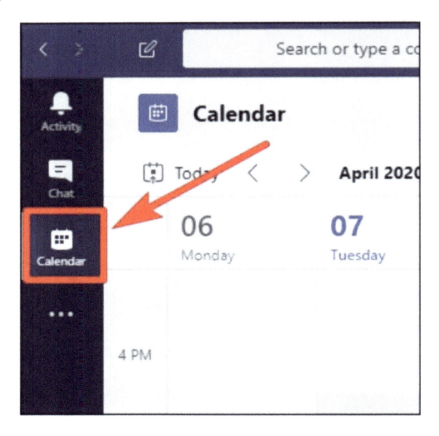

2. Click **New Meeting** at the top right.

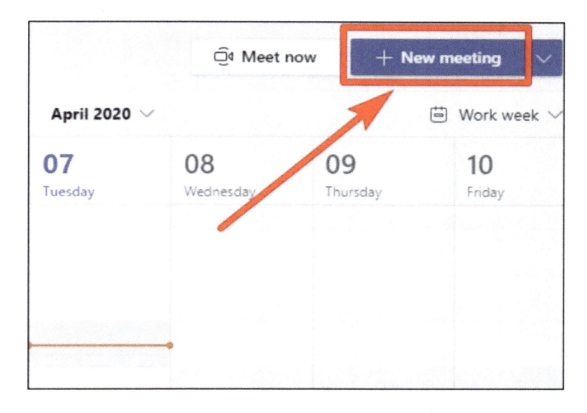

3. Fill in the meeting details:
   - **Title** – Enter a name for the meeting.
   - **Attendees** – Type names or emails to invite participants.
   - **Date & Time** – Set the start and end time.
   - **Repeat** – Choose if the meeting is a one-time event or a recurring one.
   - **Location** – Specify a physical or virtual location.
   - **Description** – Add meeting details or agenda.
4. Click **Send** to schedule the meeting.

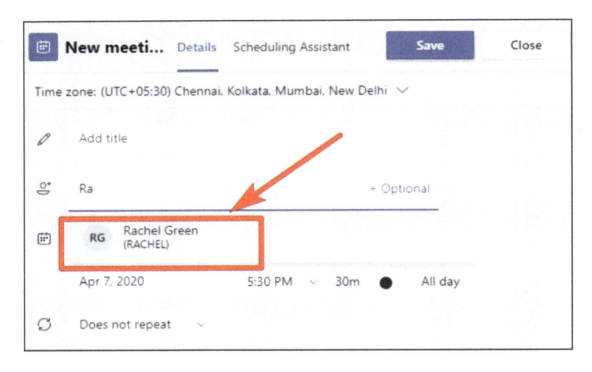

Scheduling a Meeting from a Chat or Channel

1. Open a **Chat** or **Channel**.
2. Click the **Meet Now** button (camera icon) or choose **Schedule a Meeting**.

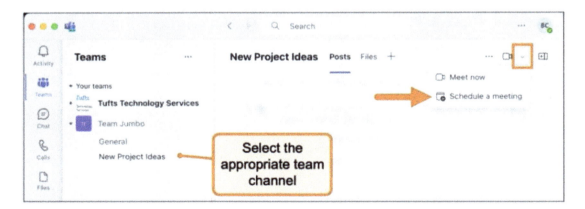

3. Set the meeting details and click **Send** to notify participants.

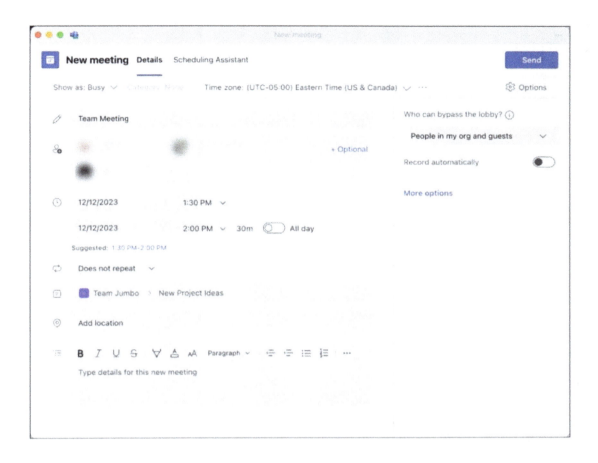

💡 **Tip:** Use the **Scheduling Assistant** in the Calendar to check availability before setting a time.

5.2 Joining a Meeting – Different Ways to Enter a Teams Meeting

Joining from the Calendar

1. Open **Microsoft Teams** and go to the **Calendar** tab.
2. Locate the scheduled meeting.
3. Click **Join** to enter the meeting.

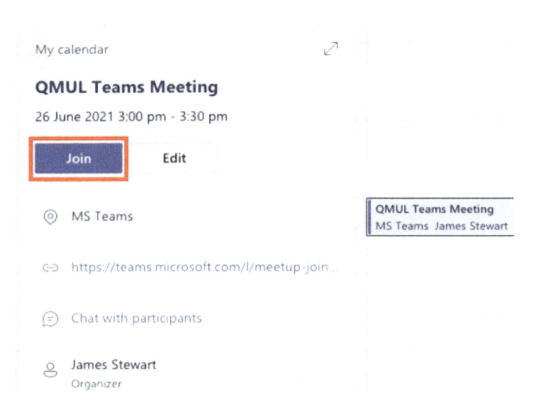

Joining from an Email Invitation

1. Open the meeting invitation email.
2. Click the **Join Microsoft Teams Meeting** link.
3. Choose to join via the **Teams app** or **web browser**.

Joining from a Chat or Channel

1. Go to the relevant **Chat** or **Channel** where the meeting is posted.
2. Click **Join** when the meeting is live.

Joining by Dialing In

- If the organizer has enabled **phone dial-in**, call the provided number and enter the access code.

💡 **Tip:** If you're having trouble with audio/video, use the **Device Settings** before joining.

5.3 Meeting Controls and Interface – Managing Participants, Mute/Unmute, Layouts, and Settings

Understanding the Meeting Interface

Once inside a meeting, you'll see the following controls at the top or bottom of your screen:

- **Mute/Unmute Microphone** – Click the **microphone icon** to toggle mute.
- **Turn Camera On/Off** – Click the **camera icon** to enable/disable video.
- **Share Screen** – Click the **Share** icon to present your screen or a specific window.
- **Raise Hand** – Click the **hand icon** to request to speak.
- **Reactions** – Use emojis to express feedback.
- **More Options (...)** – Access settings like **background effects**, **meeting notes**, and **recording**.
- **Chat** – Open the chat panel to send messages during the meeting.
- **Participants** – View and manage attendees.

Main options

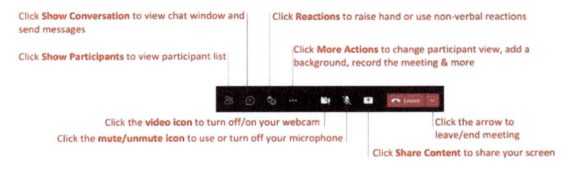

Main meeting controls

💡 **Tip:** If you're experiencing background noise, use the **Noise Suppression** feature in settings.

5.4 Managing Participants and Roles – Understanding Organizers, Presenters, and Attendees

Roles in Microsoft Teams Meetings

Organizer

- Creates and schedules the meeting.
- Has full control over meeting settings.

Presenter

- Shares screen, manages content, and moderates discussions.
- Can mute/unmute attendees.

Attendee

- Participates in the meeting but has limited control.
- Can raise hand, send chat messages, and react with emojis.

Managing Participants

1. Click the **Participants** icon during the meeting.
2. Use the options:
   - ○ **Mute All** – Silence all attendees at once.
   - ○ **Remove a Participant** – Click on their name and select **Remove**.
   - ○ **Promote/Demote Role** – Change a participant's role from attendee to presenter or vice versa.

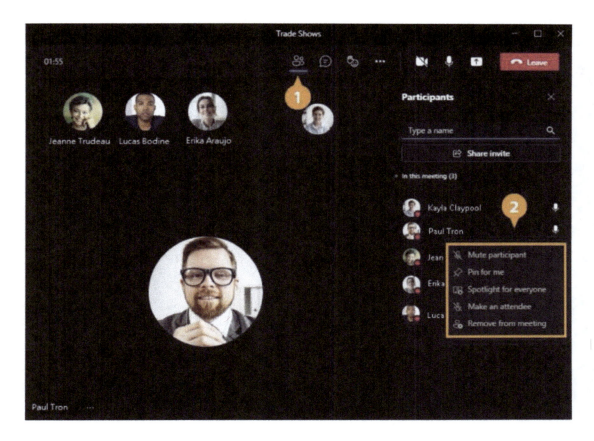

💡 **Tip:** Use the **Lobby Feature** to control who enters the meeting before it starts.

5.5 Using Meeting Chat and Reactions – Engaging with Others Without Interrupting

Using the Meeting Chat

1. Click the **Chat** icon during the meeting.
2. Type your message and press **Enter** to send.
3. Mention specific people using @name for direct messages.
4. Use formatting tools for emphasis (bold, italics, bullet points).

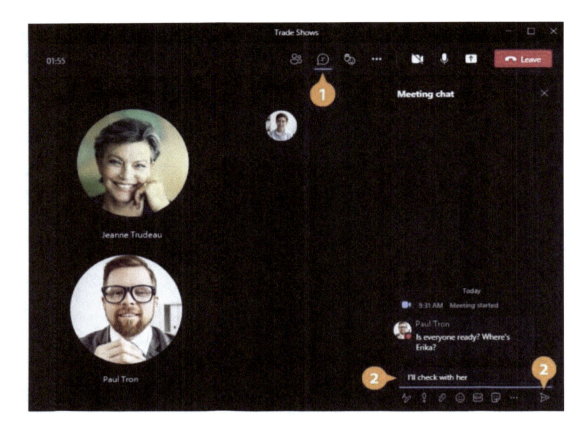

Using Reactions

- Click the **Reactions** button in the meeting toolbar.
- Choose an emoji (👍 💜 😄 😯 etc.) to provide quick feedback.

💡 **Tip:** If the chat is disabled, ask the organizer to enable it in meeting settings.

5.6 Screen Sharing and Presenting – Best Practices for Clear and Effective Presentations

How to Share Your Screen

1. Join a meeting in **Microsoft Teams**.
2. Click the **Share Screen** icon (square with an arrow) in the meeting toolbar.

3. Choose what you want to share:
   - o **Entire Screen** – Shares everything on your display.
   - o **Window** – Shares only a specific app window.
   - o **PowerPoint Live** – Uploads a PowerPoint presentation for shared control.
   - o **Whiteboard** – Opens a collaborative whiteboard for brainstorming.

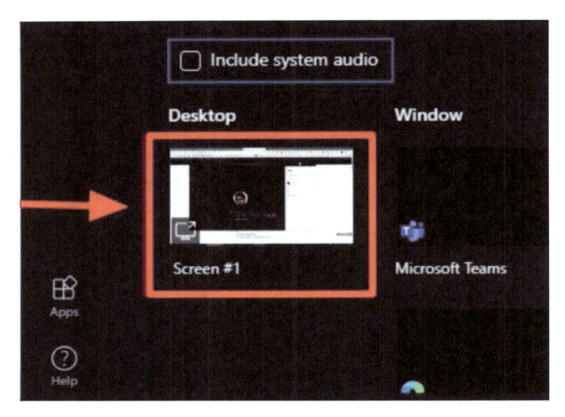

Share your full desktop screen in the meeting

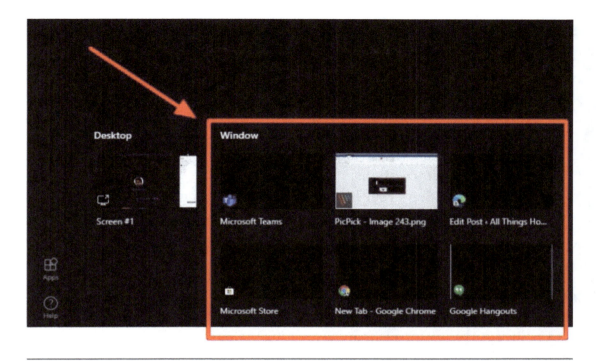

Sharing a specific window in a Microsoft Teams meeting

4. Click **Share** to begin presenting.

Best Practices for Effective Screen Sharing

- Close unnecessary apps and notifications before sharing.
- Use **PowerPoint Live** for better control over slides.
- Ensure a stable internet connection to avoid lags.
- Speak clearly and engage participants with questions.

💡 **Tip:** Use the **Laser Pointer** and **Annotations** in PowerPoint Live to make presentations more interactive.

5.7 Using Background Effects and Filters – Blur, Virtual Backgrounds, and Professional Setups

Applying a Background Effect Before a Meeting

1. Click **Join Meeting** in Microsoft Teams.
2. Before entering, click **Background Filters**.
3. Choose one of the options:
   - **Blur** – Blurs your background while keeping you in focus.
   - **Preloaded Virtual Backgrounds** – Select from available images.
   - **Custom Background** – Click **Add New** to upload an image.
4. Click **Apply** to save your selection.

Changing Background During a Meeting

1. Click **More Options (…)** in the meeting toolbar.

2. Select **Apply Background Effects**.

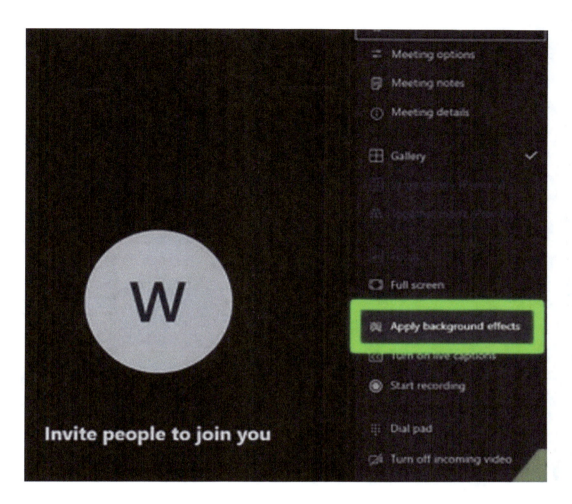

3. Choose a new background or blur effect.

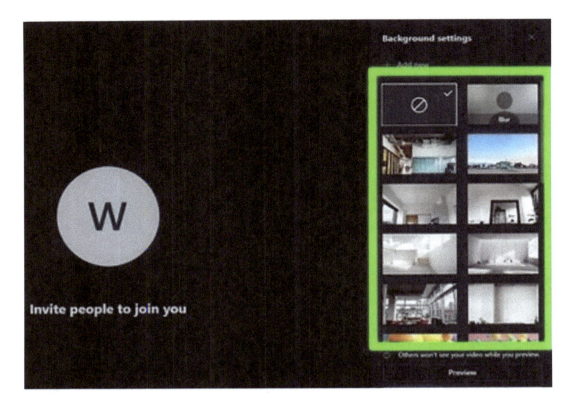

4. Click **Apply and Turn on Video**.

💡 **Tip:** For a professional setup, ensure your background is well-lit and clutter-free.

5.8 Recording Meetings – How to Save and Access Meeting Recordings

How to Record a Meeting

1. Join a **Microsoft Teams** meeting.
2. Click **More Options (...)** in the meeting toolbar.
3. Select **Start Recording**.

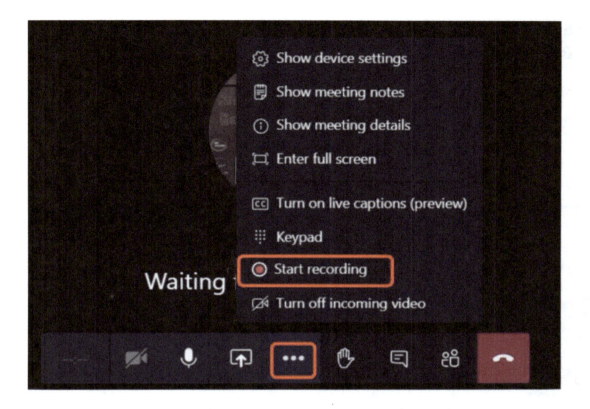

4. A banner will appear notifying all participants that the meeting is being recorded.

5. To stop recording, click **More Options (...)** again and select **Stop Recording**.

Where to Find the Recording

- Recordings are automatically saved to **OneDrive** (for private meetings) or **SharePoint** (for channel meetings).
- Access them via the **Chat** or **Files** tab in Microsoft Teams.
- The meeting organizer and those with permission can download or share the recording.

💡 **Tip:** If recording is disabled, ask your IT admin to enable it in **Teams Admin Center**.

5.9 Using Live Captions and Subtitles – Accessibility Features for Better Inclusivity

Enabling Live Captions

1. Join a **Microsoft Teams** meeting.
2. Click **More Options (…)** in the meeting toolbar.
3. Select **Turn on Live Captions**.

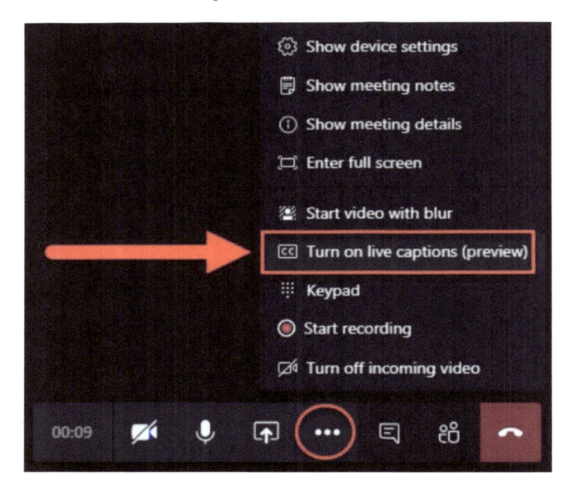

4. Captions will appear in real-time at the bottom of the screen.

Once it's on, it will transcribe what anyone says and display it as a live caption in the lower left of the meeting screen.

Once captioning is on, as people speak, the captions appear in the bottom left.

Using Live Translations for Subtitles

1. Follow the steps above to enable **Live Captions**.
2. Click **Captions Settings** and choose a preferred subtitle language.

3. Microsoft Teams will translate the spoken words into the selected language.

💡 **Tip:** Live Captions work best with clear audio. Use a good-quality microphone to improve accuracy.

5.10 Breakout Rooms in Microsoft Teams – Creating Smaller Discussion Groups Within a Meeting

Creating Breakout Rooms

1. Start a meeting as an **Organizer**.
2. Click the **Breakout Rooms** icon in the meeting toolbar.

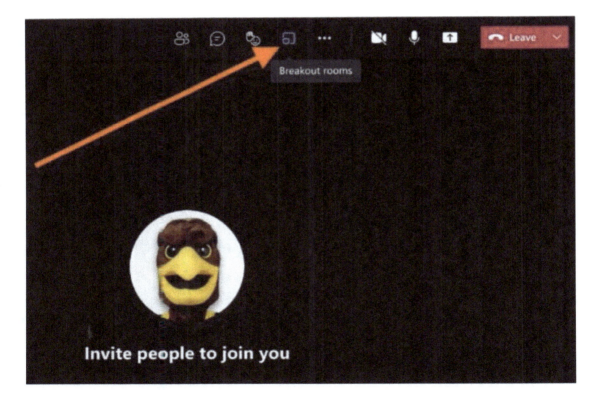

3. Choose the number of rooms you need.

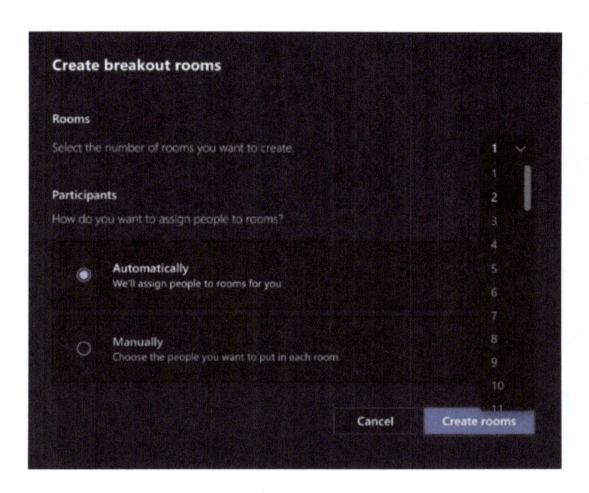

4. Assign participants automatically or manually.

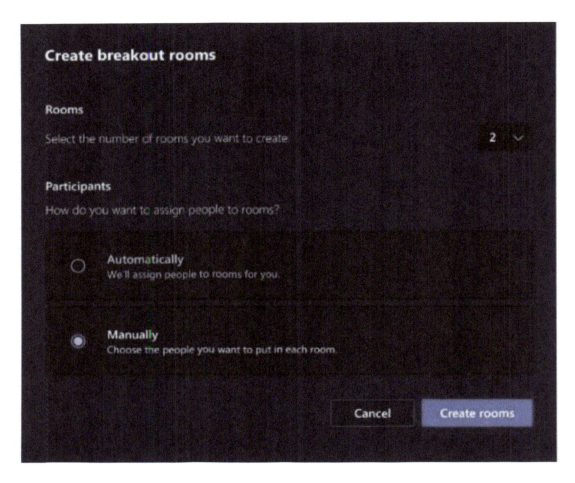

5. Click **Create Rooms**.

Managing Breakout Rooms

- Click **Open Rooms** to start the breakout sessions.
- Join any room as an organizer by selecting it from the list.
- Send announcements to all rooms by clicking **Broadcast Message**.
- Click **Close Rooms** when you're ready to bring everyone back.

💡 **Tip:** Encourage participants to use **Reactions** and **Chat** inside breakout rooms to stay engaged.

Chapter 6: File Sharing and Document Collaboration

6.1 Uploading and Sharing Files in Teams – Drag-and-Drop, OneDrive, and SharePoint

Uploading Files in Microsoft Teams

Method 1: Drag-and-Drop

1. Open the **Chat** or **Teams Channel** where you want to share a file.
2. Drag a file from your computer and drop it into the message box.
3. Click **Send** to share the file.

Method 2: Upload via the Files Tab

1. Open a **Chat** or **Teams Channel**.
2. Click the **Files** tab at the top.
3. Click **Upload** and select a file from your computer.

Method 3: Upload via OneDrive

1. In a **Chat** or **Teams Channel**, click the **Attach (paperclip icon)** in the message box.
2. Select **OneDrive** and choose a file.
3. Click **Share** to send the file.

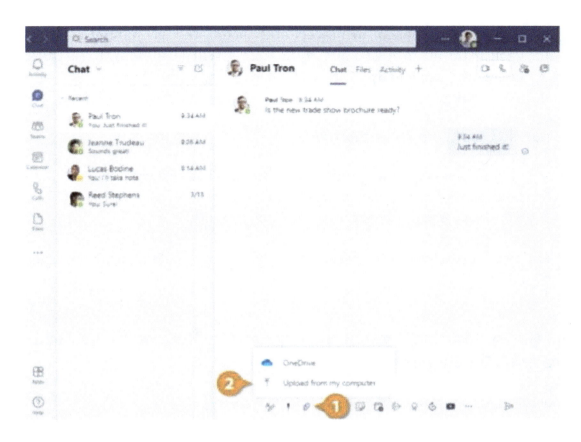

Sharing Files in Microsoft Teams

- Click the **More Options (...)** next to a file in the **Files** tab.
- Select **Copy Link** to generate a shareable link.
- Adjust sharing permissions (view/edit) and share the link.

💡 **Tip:** Use **SharePoint** for managing and collaborating on team files more efficiently.

6.2 Co-Authoring Documents in Real-Time – Working on Word, Excel, and PowerPoint Together

How to Co-Edit a Document

1. Upload a **Word, Excel, or PowerPoint** file to a **Teams Channel** or **Chat**.
2. Click on the file to open it directly in **Teams**, **Word Online**, or **Excel Online**.
3. Invite others to edit by clicking **Share** in the top-right corner.
4. Start editing together in real time.

Features of Real-Time Co-Authoring

- Multiple users can **edit simultaneously** with live cursor tracking.
- **Comments** can be added for feedback.
- **Auto-save** ensures changes are updated instantly.

💡 **Tip:** Use **@mentions** in comments to notify teammates of important updates.

6.3 Understanding Version History and File Recovery – Restoring Previous Document Versions

How to Access Version History in Microsoft Teams

1. Open the **Files** tab in a **Teams Channel** or **Chat**.
2. Locate the file and click **More Options (...)**.

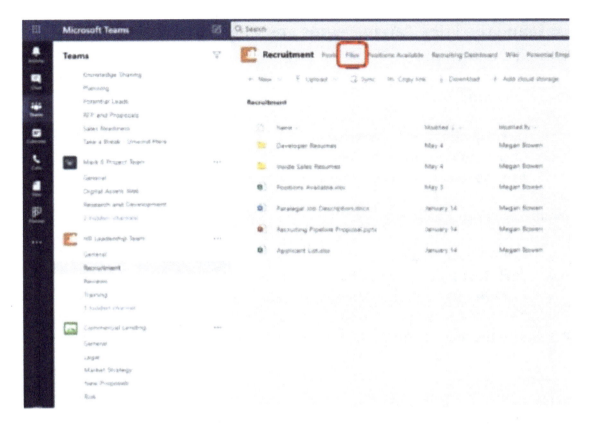

3. Select **Open in SharePoint**.
4. In SharePoint, click **Version History** to view past versions.
5. Click **Restore** on a previous version to recover it.

Recovering Deleted Files

1. Open the **Files** tab and click **Open in SharePoint**.
2. In SharePoint, click **Recycle Bin** on the left panel.
3. Locate the deleted file and click **Restore**.

💡 **Tip:** Microsoft Teams keeps file versions for a limited time. Use **OneDrive** or **SharePoint** for long-term version tracking.

6.4 Using the Files Tab in Teams and Channels – Organizing Shared Documents

Navigating the Files Tab

1. Open any **Chat** or **Teams Channel**.
2. Click the **Files** tab at the top.
3. Browse **Recent Files** or **Team Documents** stored in SharePoint.

Organizing Files Efficiently

- Use **folders** to categorize files.
- Click **Sort by** to organize by name, date, or type.
- Use **Pin to Top** for quick access to important files.

💡 Tip: Use the **Search Bar** in the **Files** tab to quickly locate specific documents.

6.5 Syncing Teams Files with OneDrive – Accessing Files Across Multiple Devices

How to Sync Teams Files with OneDrive

1. Open a **Teams Channel** and go to the **Files** tab.
2. Click **Open in SharePoint**.
3. In SharePoint, click **Sync** at the top.
4. OneDrive will open and start syncing the files to your computer.

Accessing Synced Files

- Open **File Explorer (Windows)** or **Finder (Mac)**.
- Navigate to **OneDrive – [Your Organization]**.
- Find the synced **Teams** folder under **OneDrive**.

💡 **Tip:** Synced files can be accessed offline and will update automatically when you're back online.

Chapter 7: Productivity and App Integrations

7.1 Using Microsoft Planner and To-Do in Teams – Task Management Tools for Better Workflow

Microsoft Planner in Teams

Planner helps teams collaborate and manage tasks within Microsoft Teams.

How to Add Microsoft Planner to a Team

1. Open **Microsoft Teams** and navigate to a **Team** or **Channel**.
2. Click the **+ (Add a Tab)** button at the top.
3. Select **Tasks by Planner and To-Do**.

4. Click **Create a New Plan** or select an existing one.

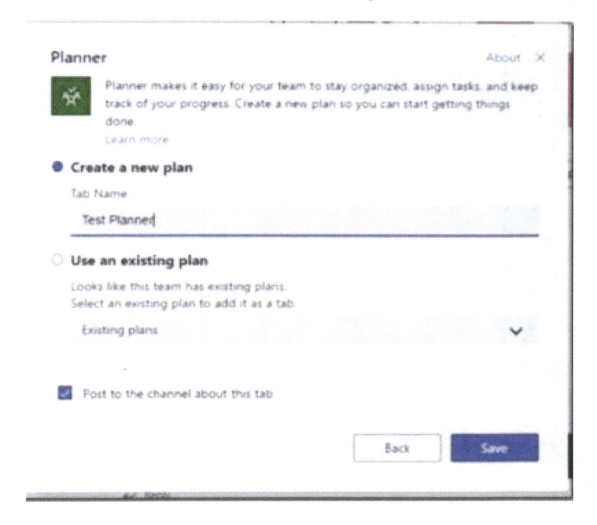

5. Name the plan and click **Save**.

Creating and Assigning Tasks in Planner

1. Open the **Tasks** tab in your Team.
2. Click **Add Task** and enter a task name.

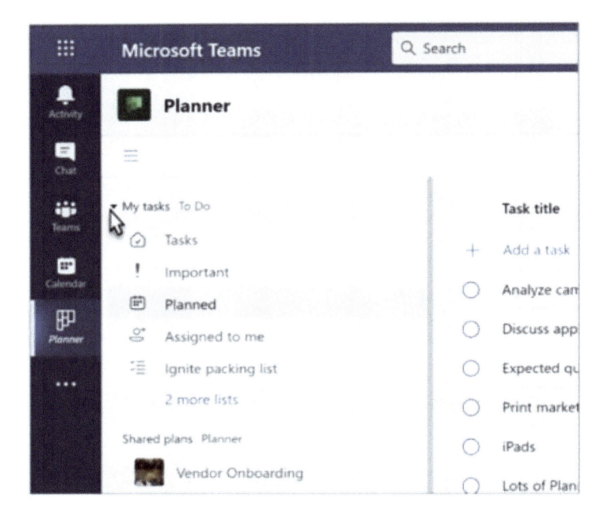

3. Set a **due date** and **assign** it to a team member.
4. Click **Add Task** to save.

💡 **Tip:** Use **Buckets** in Planner to categorize tasks into groups like "To Do," "In Progress," and "Completed."

Microsoft To-Do in Teams

To-Do is a personal task manager that syncs across devices.

How to Access Microsoft To-Do in Teams

1. Click the **Apps** icon in the left sidebar.
2. Search for **Tasks by Planner and To-Do** and click **Add**.
3. Open **My Tasks** to see personal To-Do lists and Planner tasks assigned to you.

💡 **Tip:** Use **Reminders** and **Recurring Tasks** in To-Do to stay on track.

7.2 Adding and Using Third-Party Apps – Integrating Trello, Asana, Zoom, and More

How to Add Third-Party Apps in Microsoft Teams

1. Click **Apps** in the left sidebar.
2. Search for the app you want to integrate (e.g., **Trello, Asana, Zoom**).
3. Click **Add** to install the app.

Popular App Integrations

Trello (Task Management)

- Add Trello to a Team by clicking **+ (Add a Tab)** > **Trello**.
- Log in to your Trello account and select a board to display in Teams.

Asana (Project Management)

- Install Asana from the **Apps** section.
- Connect to your Asana account and view tasks directly in Teams.

Zoom (Video Conferencing)

- Install Zoom from **Apps**.
- Click **Sign In** and authorize Teams to use your Zoom account.
- Start or schedule Zoom meetings directly within Teams.

Tip: Use **Connectors** in Teams to receive updates from third-party apps in your channels.

7.3 Creating and Managing Forms and Surveys – Collecting Feedback in Teams

How to Create a Microsoft Form in Teams

1. Open a **Chat** or **Channel**.
2. Click **+ (Add a Tab)** and select **Forms**.

Find the Microsoft Forms app and click it:

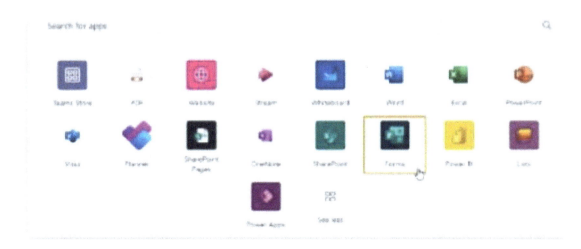

3. Click **Create a New Form** and enter a title and description.
4. Add **multiple-choice, text, rating, or date** questions.
5. Click **Send** to share the form.

How to Collect and View Responses

1. Open the **Forms** tab in your Team.
2. Click the form to view **Responses**.
3. Download results as an **Excel file** for analysis.

💡 **Tip:** Use **Microsoft Forms Polls** in meetings to gather quick feedback.

7.4 Using Whiteboard for Brainstorming – Visual Collaboration Tools in Meetings

How to Access Microsoft Whiteboard in Teams

1. Start a **Teams Meeting**.
2. Click the **Share Content** button.

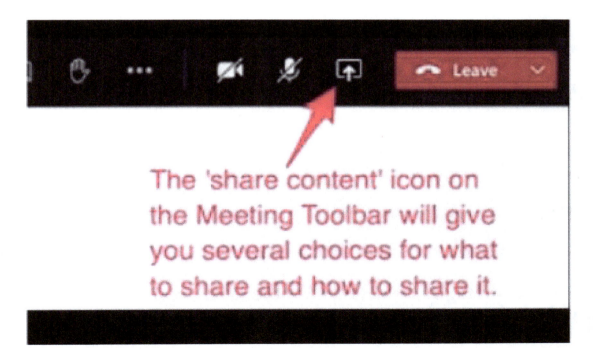

The 'share content' icon on the Meeting Toolbar will give you several choices for what to share and how to share it.

3. Select **Microsoft Whiteboard**.

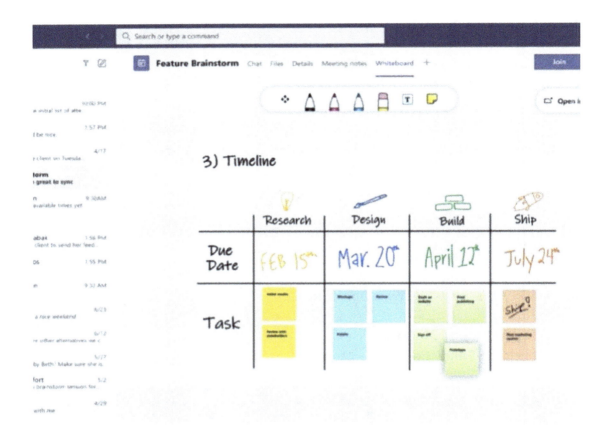

Features of Microsoft Whiteboard

- Draw, write, and add sticky notes.
- Insert images and diagrams.
- Collaborate in real-time with team members.

💡 **Tip:** Use **Templates** in Whiteboard for structured brainstorming sessions.

7.5 Automating Tasks with Power Automate – Making Teams Work Smarter for You

What is Power Automate?

Power Automate (formerly Microsoft Flow) automates repetitive tasks in Teams.

How to Create an Automated Workflow in Teams

1. Open **Microsoft Teams** and click **Apps**.
2. Search for **Power Automate** and click **Add**.
3. Click **Create Flow** and select a template (e.g., "Post a message in Teams when a file is uploaded to OneDrive").
4. Customize the flow and click **Save**.

Examples of Automated Workflows

- Get **email notifications** when a new Teams file is uploaded.
- Auto-post daily updates to a Teams **Channel**.
- Sync tasks between **Microsoft To-Do and Planner**.

💡 **Tip:** Use **Pre-Built Templates** in Power Automate to save time.

Chapter 8: Security, Privacy, and Admin Controls

8.1 Understanding Permissions and Access Levels – Managing User Roles Effectively

User Roles in Microsoft Teams

Microsoft Teams has three primary roles:

1. **Owner** – Manages team settings, adds or removes members, and controls permissions.
2. **Member** – Participates in team activities, creates and edits content, but has limited administrative control.
3. **Guest** – External users who have restricted access to team resources.

How to Manage Permissions in Teams

Changing Team Member Roles

1. Open **Microsoft Teams** and go to the **Teams** tab.
2. Select the team you want to manage.
3. Click **More Options (⋯)** > **Manage Team**.

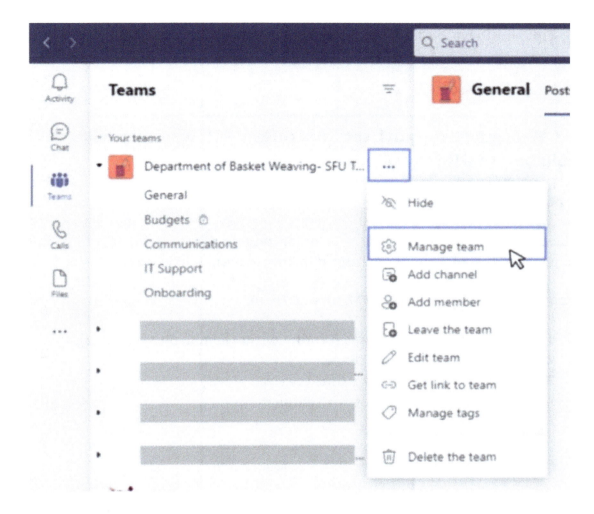

4. Under **Members**, find the user you want to modify.
5. Click the dropdown next to their name and select **Owner, Member, or Guest**.

Managing Channel Permissions

1. Open the team and select a **Channel**.
2. Click **More Options (···) > Manage Channel**.
3. Adjust settings such as **who can post messages** and **who can moderate the channel**.

💡 **Tip:** Use **Private Channels** for sensitive discussions that only selected team members should access.

8.2 Managing External Users and Guests – How to Securely Collaborate with Outsiders

Who Are Guest Users in Teams?

Guest users are people outside your organization who can participate in Teams conversations, calls, and file sharing with limited permissions.

How to Enable Guest Access in Microsoft Teams

1. Open the **Microsoft Teams Admin Center** (admin.microsoft.com).
2. Click **Teams > Manage Teams**.
3. Go to **Org-wide settings > Guest access**.
4. Toggle **Allow guest access in Teams** to **On**.
5. Click **Save**.

How to Add a Guest to a Team

1. Open **Microsoft Teams** and go to the **Teams** tab.
2. Select the team where you want to add a guest.
3. Click **More Options (⋯) > Add Member**.
4. Enter the guest's **email address**.
5. Click **Add**, then select **Guest** as their role.
6. Click **Done**.

💡 **Tip:** Guests can't access certain features like **OneDrive sync**, **Planner**, or **organization-wide teams**.

8.3 Setting Up Two-Factor Authentication – Enhancing Account Security

What is Two-Factor Authentication (2FA)?

2FA adds an extra layer of security by requiring both a **password** and a **verification code** sent to a mobile device or email.

How to Enable Two-Factor Authentication for Microsoft Teams

1. Sign in to **Microsoft 365 Admin Center** (admin.microsoft.com).
2. Click **Users > Active Users**.
3. Select the user account you want to secure.
4. Click **Manage Multi-Factor Authentication**.
5. Select the user and click **Enable**.
6. Click **Enforce** to require 2FA for that account.

How to Set Up 2FA for Your Own Account

1. Open **Microsoft Teams** and go to **Settings**.
2. Click **Security & Privacy > Two-Step Verification**.
3. Select **Enable Two-Step Verification**.
4. Choose a verification method:
   - **Authenticator app** (recommended)
   - **SMS code**
   - **Email verification**
5. Follow the on-screen setup instructions.

💡 **Tip:** Use the **Microsoft Authenticator app** for a seamless 2FA experience.

8.4 Data Protection and Compliance in Microsoft Teams – Microsoft's Security Policies and How They Affect Users

How Microsoft Protects Your Data

Microsoft Teams follows strict security policies to ensure data protection, including:

- **End-to-end encryption** for chats and calls.
- **Data Loss Prevention (DLP)** to prevent sharing sensitive information.
- **Compliance with GDPR, HIPAA, and ISO 27001** security standards.

How to Secure Files and Conversations in Teams

Using Sensitivity Labels

1. Open **Microsoft Teams Admin Center**.
2. Click **Security & Compliance** > **Sensitivity Labels**.
3. Click **Create a Label** and define access policies.
4. Apply labels to files and chats to restrict access.

Setting Up Data Loss Prevention (DLP) Policies

1. Open **Microsoft 365 Compliance Center**.
2. Click **Data Loss Prevention** > **Create a Policy**.
3. Choose a template (e.g., **Protect Credit Card Data**).
4. Select **Microsoft Teams** as the service to apply the policy.
5. Define rules for detecting and blocking sensitive information sharing.

💡 **Tip:** Use **Conditional Access Policies** to restrict Teams access based on device or location.

Chapter 9: Microsoft Teams for Specific Use Cases

9.1 Microsoft Teams for Business – Managing Company-Wide Communication and Collaboration

Why Businesses Use Microsoft Teams

Microsoft Teams is a powerful tool for **business communication, collaboration, and productivity**, offering features such as:

- **Team-based chat and file sharing** to enhance collaboration.
- **Virtual meetings and webinars** to connect with employees and clients.
- **Task management** with Microsoft Planner and To-Do.
- **Integration with business tools** like SharePoint, OneDrive, and Power Automate.

Setting Up Microsoft Teams for Business

Step 1: Create a Team for Your Organization

1. Open **Microsoft Teams** and click on the **Teams** tab.
2. Click **Join or create a team > Create a team**.
3. Choose **From scratch** or **From an existing Microsoft 365 group**.
4. Select **Private** (for internal use) or **Public** (for open collaboration).
5. Name your team and add a description.
6. Click **Create**, then **Add members** to invite employees.

Step 2: Set Up Company-Wide Channels

1. Go to your **newly created team**.
2. Click **More Options (⋯) > Add Channel**.

3. Name the channel (e.g., **Company Announcements, HR, Sales, IT Support**).
4. Choose **Standard** (visible to all team members) or **Private** (restricted access).
5. Click **Create**.

Step 3: Managing Company Communication

- Use **Announcements** in the **General** channel to share important updates.
- Utilize **@mentions** to notify specific teams or employees.
- Organize **virtual meetings** using the Calendar tab.

💡 **Tip:** Use **Live Events** in Teams to host company-wide town halls and presentations.

9.2 Microsoft Teams for Education – Using Teams for Virtual Classrooms, Assignments, and Grading

Why Educators Use Microsoft Teams

Microsoft Teams for Education provides a **digital learning environment**, enabling:

- **Virtual classrooms** with video meetings and chat.
- **Assignments and quizzes** with Microsoft Forms.
- **Collaboration tools** like OneNote Class Notebook.

Setting Up Microsoft Teams for a Classroom

Step 1: Create a Class Team

1. Open **Microsoft Teams** and click **Teams**.
2. Click **Join or create a team > Create a team**.
3. Select **Class**.

4. Enter a **Class Name** (e.g., **Grade 8 Math**) and description.
5. Click **Next** and **Add Students** (or skip to add later).

Step 2: Organizing Lessons with Channels

- Create **subject-specific channels** (e.g., **Homework Help, Discussions, Announcements**).
- Use **Files tab** to share study materials.
- Assign **moderation roles** to students for structured discussions.

Step 3: Assigning and Grading Work

1. Go to the **Assignments** tab.
2. Click **Create Assignment**.
3. Add **instructions, due dates, and files**.
4. Click **Assign** to distribute it to students.
5. Use the **Grades tab** to track and review submissions.

💡 **Tip:** Enable **Reading Progress** to help students improve reading fluency with AI-driven insights.

9.3 Microsoft Teams for Healthcare – How Hospitals and Medical Professionals Use Teams for Patient Communication

Why Healthcare Providers Use Microsoft Teams

Microsoft Teams helps hospitals and clinics with:

- **Secure patient communication** (HIPAA-compliant chat and video calls).
- **Collaboration among medical staff** (Doctors, Nurses, Admins).
- **Integration with electronic health records (EHRs)** for quick access to patient information.

Setting Up Microsoft Teams for Healthcare

Step 1: Enable Healthcare-Specific Features

1. Open **Microsoft Teams Admin Center**.
2. Go to **Manage Teams > Healthcare Settings**.
3. Enable **Virtual Rounding, Secure Messaging, and Shift Scheduling**.
4. Configure compliance settings for **HIPAA** or other regulations.

Step 2: Using Teams for Patient Appointments

1. Go to **Calendar** and schedule a **Virtual Visit**.
2. Invite **patients or external doctors** via email.
3. Use **Meeting Notes** to document consultations securely.
4. Share medical records through **OneDrive or SharePoint** (if allowed).

Step 3: Managing Medical Staff Communication

- Create **specialty-specific teams** (e.g., **Cardiology, Pediatrics, Emergency Care**).
- Use **Shift Scheduling** to manage doctor and nurse rotations.
- Enable **Priority Notifications** to alert medical staff about urgent messages.

💡 **Tip:** Use **Microsoft Bookings** to schedule and manage patient consultations efficiently.

9.4 Microsoft Teams for Personal Use – Staying Connected with Friends and Family

Why Use Microsoft Teams for Personal Communication?

Microsoft Teams isn't just for work—it's a great tool for:

- **Video calls with family and friends**.

- **Group chats for planning events and sharing updates**.
- **Sharing photos, videos, and files** securely.

Getting Started with Microsoft Teams for Personal Use

Step 1: Create a Personal Account

1. Download **Microsoft Teams** on **desktop or mobile**.
2. Open the app and select **Sign Up for Free**.
3. Choose **For personal use**.
4. Enter your **Microsoft account email** and create a password.
5. Verify your email and sign in.

Step 2: Starting a Video Call

1. Open **Microsoft Teams** and go to **Chat**.
2. Click **New Chat** and enter a contact's name or email.
3. Click the **Video Call icon** to start a call.
4. Use **screen sharing** to show photos, documents, or slides.

Step 3: Creating a Family or Friends Group

1. Open **Teams** and go to **Chat**.
2. Click **New Group Chat** and add contacts.
3. Name the group (e.g., **Weekend Plans, Family Updates**).
4. Start chatting, sharing files, and scheduling meetups.

💡 **Tip:** Use **Together Mode** in video calls for a more immersive group experience.

Chapter 10: Advanced Features and Expert Tips

10.1 Keyboard Shortcuts for Power Users – Speeding Up Your Workflow

Keyboard shortcuts help you navigate Microsoft Teams faster. Here are the most useful ones:

General Shortcuts

- **Ctrl + N** – Start a new chat
- **Ctrl + E** – Go to the search bar
- **Ctrl + /** – View all shortcuts

Meeting and Call Shortcuts

- **Ctrl + Shift + M** – Mute/unmute your microphone
- **Ctrl + Shift + O** – Turn camera on/off
- **Ctrl + Shift + K** – Raise/lower hand

Chat and Messaging Shortcuts

- **Ctrl + Shift + X** – Expand message box
- **Ctrl + Enter** – Send message
- **Alt + ↑ / ↓** – Navigate between messages

💡 **Tip:** Use **Alt + Shift + D** to open the **Calendar** quickly.

10.2 Hidden Features and Lesser-Known Tips – Tricks to Improve Efficiency

1. Message Bookmarking with "Save This Message"

- Hover over a message, click **More options (···)** > **Save this message**.
- Access saved messages via **/saved** in the search bar.

2. Using Slash Commands for Quick Actions

Type these in the search bar for faster navigation:

- **/files** – View recent files
- **/call [name]** – Start a call
- **/goto [team or channel]** – Jump to a team or channel

3. Immersive Reader for Distraction-Free Reading

- Click **More options (···)** on a message > **Immersive Reader**.
- Adjust text size, font, and background for better focus.

10.3 Troubleshooting Common Issues – Solving Audio, Video, and Connection Problems

1. Fixing Audio Problems

- Ensure **microphone access** is enabled in **Windows Settings** > **Privacy & Security** > **Microphone**.
- Select the correct microphone in **Teams Settings** > **Devices**.

2. Fixing Video Issues

- Check if the camera is being used by another app (e.g., Zoom or Skype).
- Update camera drivers via **Device Manager** > **Cameras**.

3. Solving Connection Issues

- Run the **Teams Network Diagnostic Tool**
  (https://aka.ms/teamsnetworkcheck).
- Switch to a wired connection or **restart your router**.

💡 **Tip:** Clear the **Teams Cache** to fix performance issues:

1. Close Teams.
2. Delete %AppData%\Microsoft\Teams\Cache.
3. Restart Teams.

10.4 Customizing Notifications and Alerts – Preventing Distractions While Staying Informed

1. Changing Notification Settings

1. Click your **profile picture** > **Settings** > **Notifications**.
2. Adjust alerts for messages, mentions, and reactions.

2. Setting Up Quiet Hours (Mobile)

1. Open **Teams Mobile App** > Tap **Settings** > **Notifications**.
2. Enable **Quiet Hours** and set a schedule.

3. Using Do Not Disturb Mode

1. Type **/dnd** in the search bar to enable.
2. Type **/available** to turn off.

💡 **Tip:** Use **Priority Contacts** to allow important messages through DND.

10.5 Using Microsoft Teams on Mobile Devices – How to Use Teams Effectively on Smartphones and Tablets

1. Downloading and Setting Up the Mobile App

- Available on **iOS** and **Android**.
- Sign in with your **Microsoft 365 account**.

2. Key Features on Mobile

- **Swipe Left on Chats** – Mark messages as unread.
- **Tap & Hold Messages** – Quick reply or react.
- **Join Meetings with One Tap** – Tap calendar events to join instantly.

3. Sharing Files and Media on the Go

- Use **OneDrive integration** to share files quickly.
- Send **voice messages** for faster communication.

💡 **Tip:** Enable **Dark Mode** for better visibility and battery life.

Index

www.ingramcontent.com/pod-product-compliance
Lightning Source LLC
LaVergne TN
LVHW080118070326
832902LV00015B/2650